*For Flavia and Richard – my guiding stars,
and for Joseph – my desert oasis.*

– C.W

To our Moms.

– Muti

First edition published in 2025 by Flying Eye Books Ltd.
27 Westgate Street, London, E8 3RL.

Text © Christina Webb 2025
Illustrations © Muti 2025

Edited by Sara Forster

1 3 5 7 9 10 8 6 4 2

Published in the US by Flying Eye Books Ltd.
Printed in China on FSC® certified paper.

ISBN: 978-1-83874-180-8
www.flyingeyebooks.com

CHRISTINA WEBB

MUTI

EARTH'S INCREDIBLE PLACES
THE SAHARA

FLYING EYE BOOKS

CONTENTS

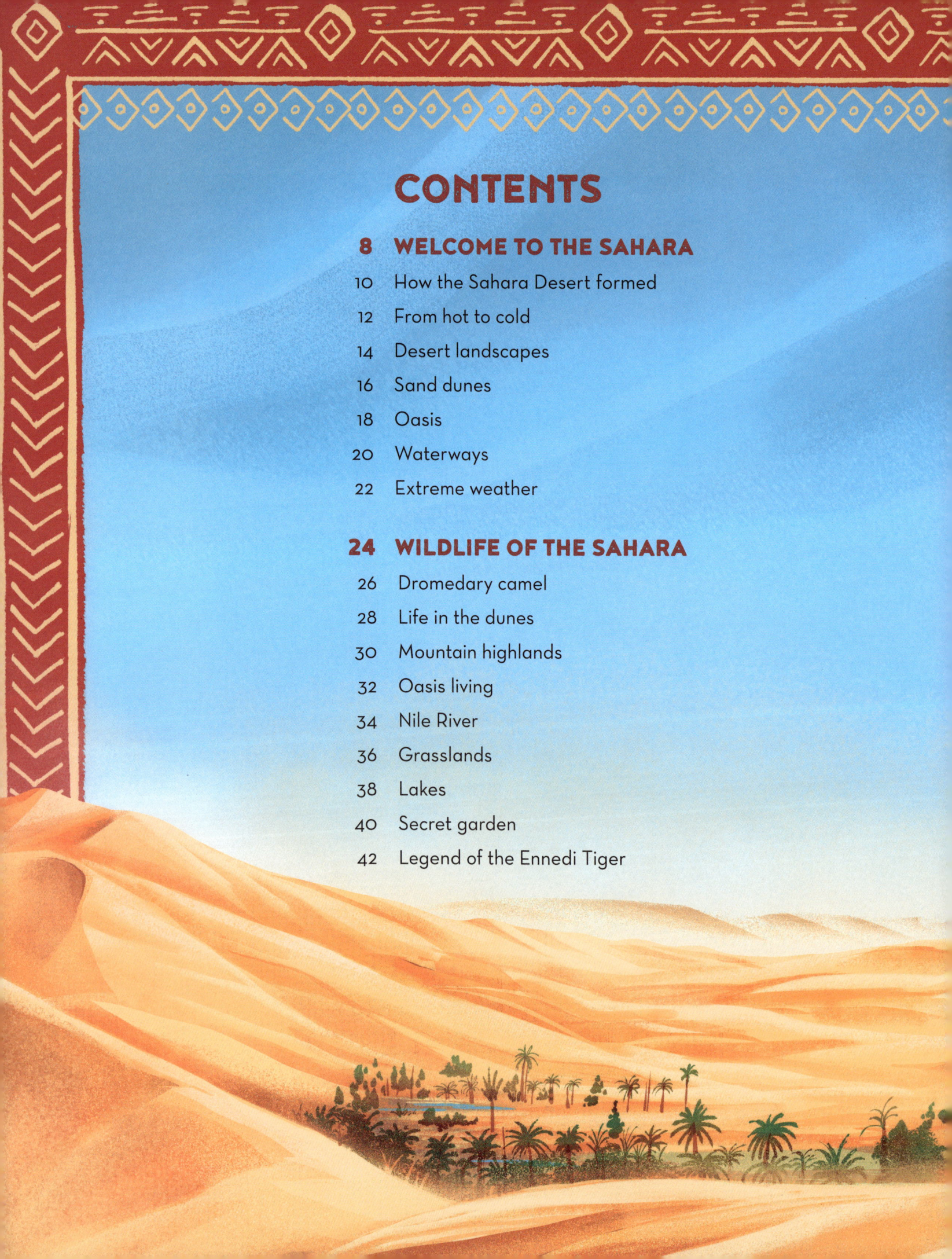

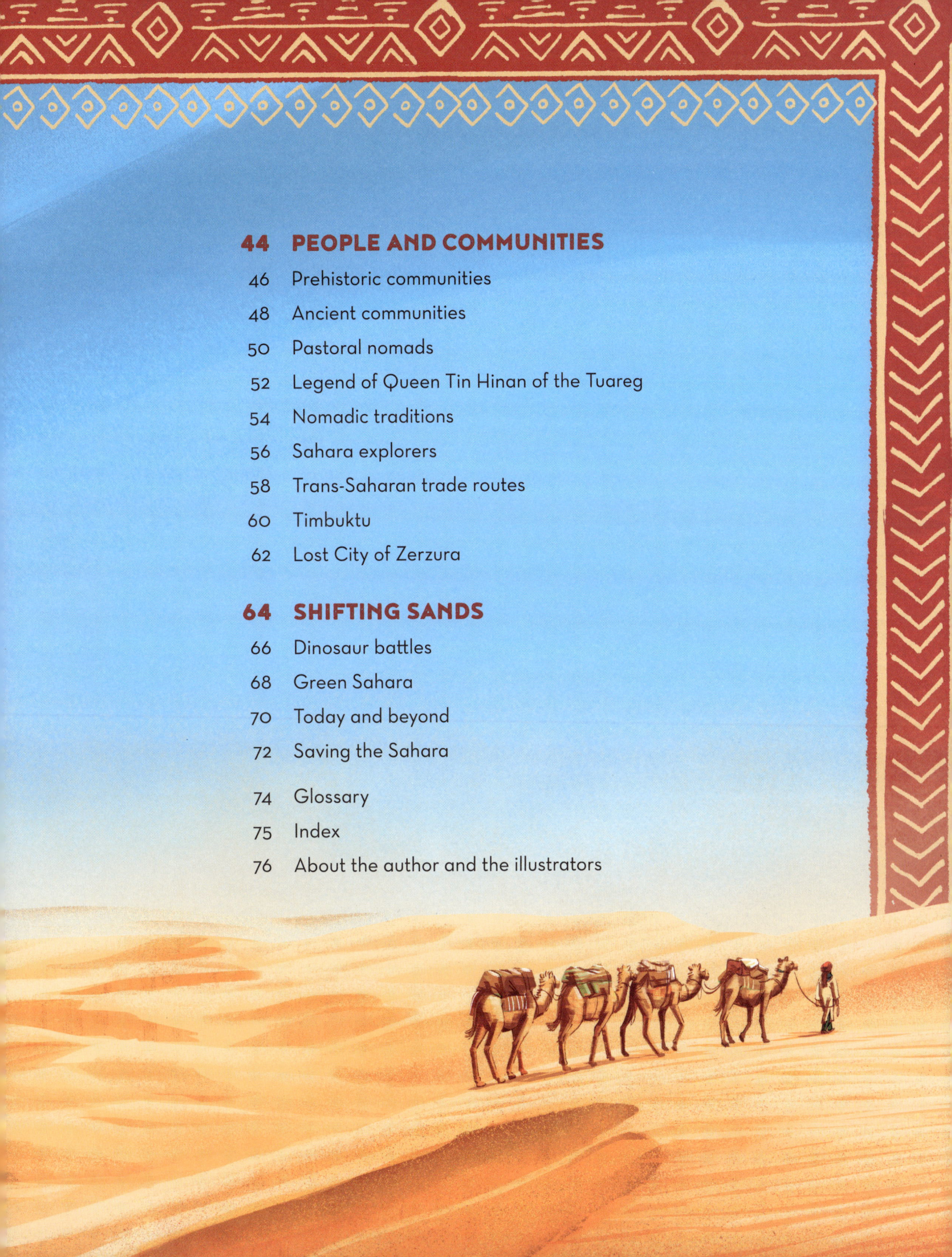

WELCOME TO THE SAHARA

Touching almost every corner of North Africa is a land where sand reigns and water is as precious as gold. A land where dunes sing and shimmering mirages bounce off the hazy horizon.

You are about to discover one of the wildest habitats on Earth, where life thrives against all odds. Where river crocodiles glide, ostriches sprint, scorpions burrow and oasis pools glisten. This is a land where pharaohs and queens once ruled, and traders journeyed with trinkets in tow. Where caves preserve paintings of a greener past, and soils reveal relics of forgotten beasts that roamed the land.

Here, time seems to stand still, yet nomadic people are always moving. Days are spent under the glare of the searing sun, while nights dip below freezing. Between droughts there are floods.

This is the Sahara Desert, a land of extremes where only the tough survive...

HOW THE SAHARA DESERT FORMED

The Sahara is the world's largest hot desert. Sweeping across a colossal 9.4 million square km, it's almost as big as the United States!

THE SAHARAN RANGE

The desert blankets the entire northerly African continent, from Cairo in the east to Casablanca in the west. It covers portions of 10 countries, as well as the Western Sahara territory.

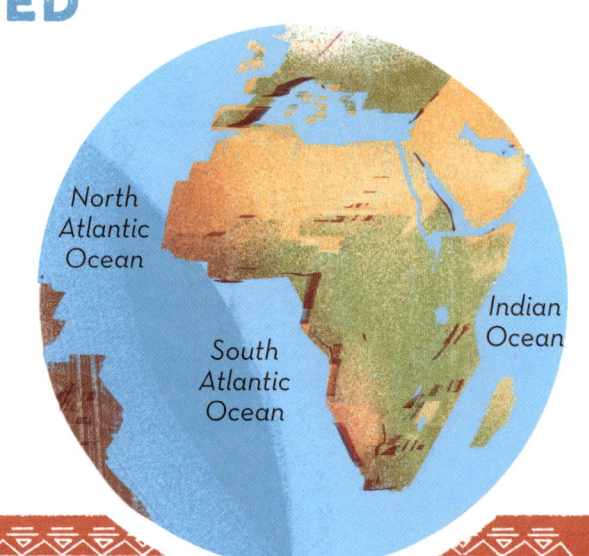

North Atlantic Ocean

South Atlantic Ocean

Indian Ocean

MOROCCO

TUNISIA

LIBYA

EGYPT

WESTERN SAHARA

ALGERIA

MAURITANIA

MALI

NIGER

CHAD

SUDAN

CLIMATE CYCLE

The Sahara's climate is forever changing. It has a climate cycle, which means it goes through humid (wet) and arid (dry) periods that last for thousands of years. These are caused by changes in the Earth's axis (tilt) – when it shifts, it alters the amount of sunlight that reaches the Earth. When more sunlight beams down on a region, it undergoes a dry period, which is what the Sahara is currently experiencing.

THE SEA THAT DISAPPEARED

Once upon a time, the Sahara was part of a great sea. To understand how it evolved into a desert, we need to go way, way back... Our story begins 250 million years ago, with an enormous body of water called the Tethys Sea.

1

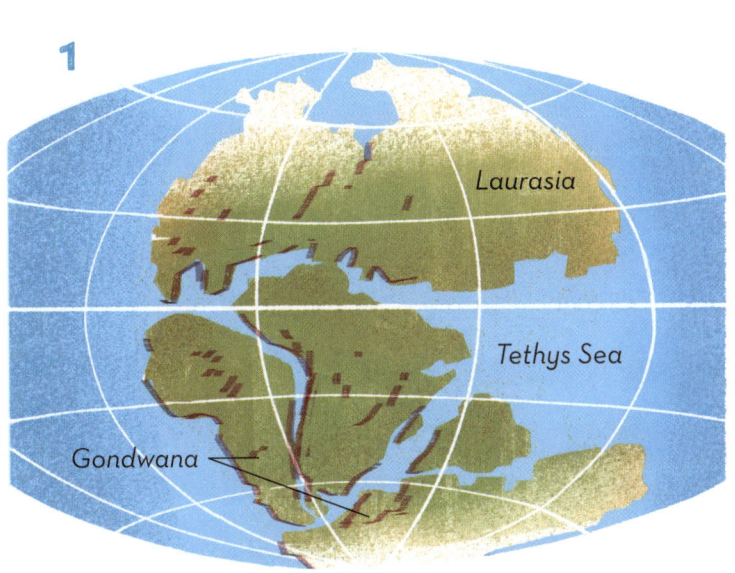

Laurasia

Tethys Sea

Gondwana

2

Mediterranean Sea

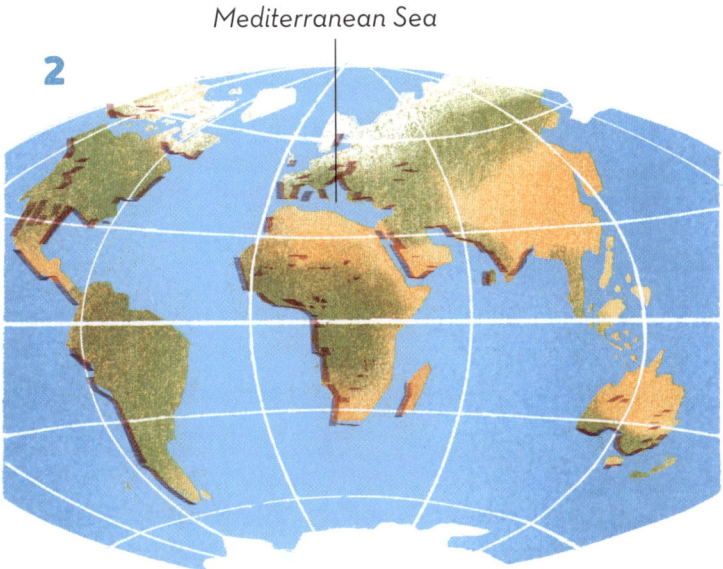

The continents looked very different to today, and this vast channel of water split supercontinents Laurasia and Gondwana in two – running all the way from the Atlantic to the Indian Ocean.

The Tethys Sea began to shrink when the two continents shifted and then collided. It was reduced to the much smaller Mediterranean Sea we recognise today.

3

The formation of the Atlas Mountains in North Africa 30 million years ago also played a part in the drying out of the Sahara. The mighty mountain range acts as a shield, preventing the damp ocean winds from reaching the inner desert.

Water reflects more sunlight than land, so when the land replaced the sea it absorbed more heat from the sun. The area also saw less rain due to a dry period, and so it eventually became a hot, dry desert environment.

FROM HOT TO COLD

Daytime, and the desert air sizzles with heat. Night-time, and it whispers an icy breath. With Saharan temperatures swinging dramatically between hot and cold, it's hard to believe that its days and nights exist in the same place.

WHY ARE DAYTIMES HOT?

Between May and September, the Sahara Desert is the hottest region in the world. Daytime temperatures can rocket up to a blistering 50°C.

WHY ARE NIGHTTIMES COLD?

After the sun sets, temperatures can plummet to well below freezing.

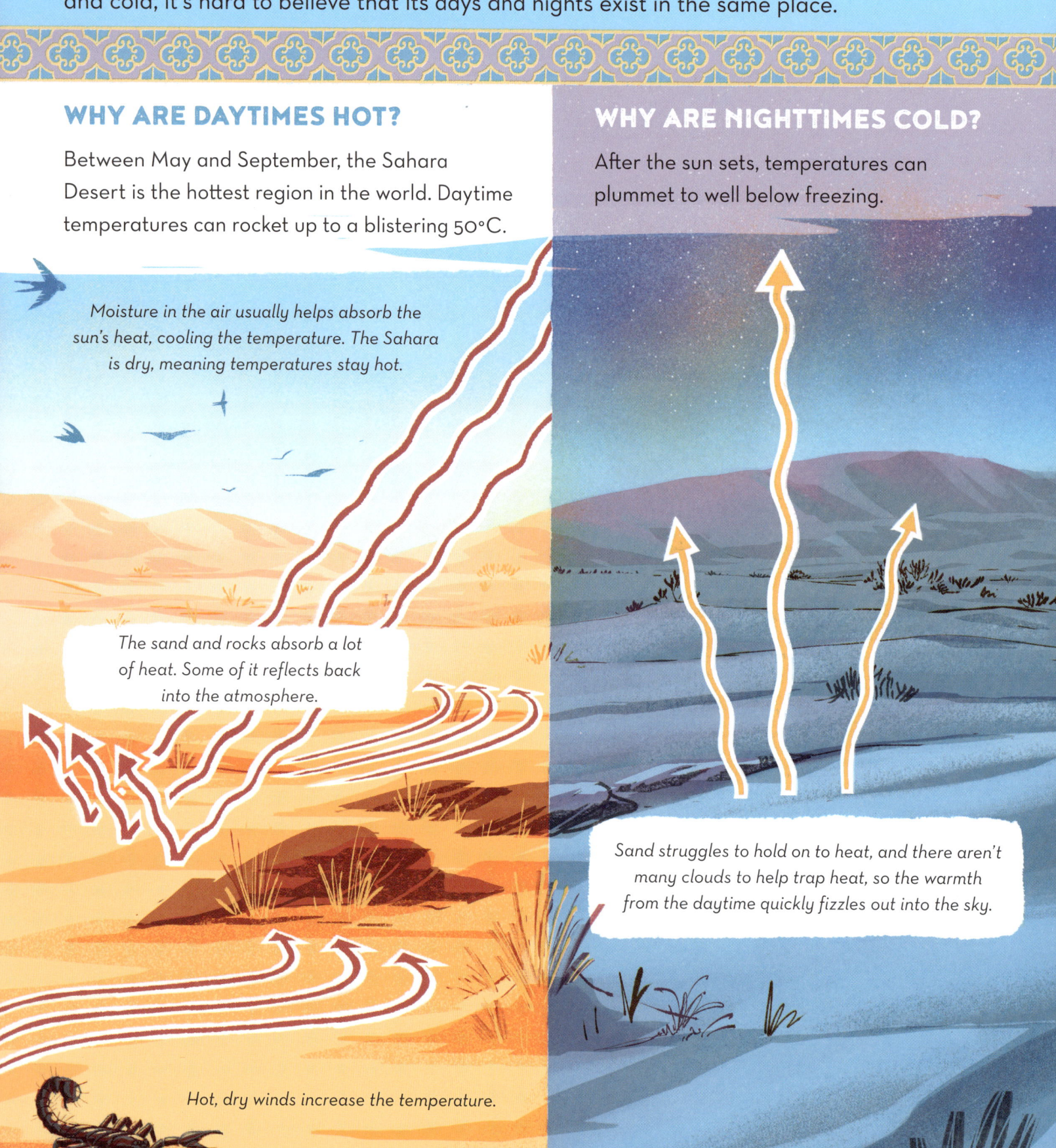

Moisture in the air usually helps absorb the sun's heat, cooling the temperature. The Sahara is dry, meaning temperatures stay hot.

The sand and rocks absorb a lot of heat. Some of it reflects back into the atmosphere.

Sand struggles to hold on to heat, and there aren't many clouds to help trap heat, so the warmth from the daytime quickly fizzles out into the sky.

Hot, dry winds increase the temperature.

DRIED OUT

Deserts are the driest environments in the world. The parched Saharan earth receives just a trickle of rain each year, soaking up an average of 3 mm.

SNOW-CAPPED SKI SLOPES

Soft layers of snow cloak the northern Saharan mountaintops in winter months. There is even enough snow falling over Morocco's Atlas Mountains to allow for skiing! The Oukaïmeden Ski Resort is located near Marrakesh; its highest mountains reach 3,200 metres high.

DESERT LANDSCAPES

If you are adventurous enough to navigate the Sahara Desert (and come well-prepared!), you'll cross vast landscapes of regs, hamadas, sand dunes and mountains that seem to go on forever.

REGS AND HAMADAS

Most people think that the Sahara is mostly sandy, but in fact, 70 per cent of the desert is made up of rocky terrain called *regs* and *hamadas*.

Regs are remnants of rivers and seabeds and are made up of sand and gravel. Travelling over their barren, rocky surfaces can feel as if you're walking on the moon.

A hamada is a rocky plateau (a flat surface of raised land). Tinrhert is a hamada in the Algerian Sahara that sits at 550 metres above sea level.

EYE OF AFRICA

It's no surprise that the ancient Saharan landscape is home to some unusual formations. Known as the 'Eye of Africa', the Richat Structure in Mauritania is an enormous spiral that looks like a gigantic seashell made of rocks. Geologists believe it was formed by the erosion of a dome-shaped rock over millions of years. At 40 km wide, it can be seen from outer space! Astronauts would use it as a point of reference when floating through the cosmos.

MOUNTAINS

Mountains only make up a small percentage of the Sahara, but lots of people live here. Ranges include Tibesti, Hoggar and the Atlas Mountains – with the latter rising from the soils of Morocco, Algeria and Tunisia. These remote corners are some of the most inaccessible places on Earth. The highest peak in the Sahara belongs to the blackened crater of Emi Koussi, a volcano in the Tibesti Mountains. It peers down from a height of 3,444 metres.

SAND DUNES

Though they are one of its most recognisable features, only a quarter of the Sahara is made up of sweeping, drifting sand dunes.

HOW SAND DUNES FORM

As the wind blows across the desert it sculpts loose sand into mounds, ridges and hills that we call sand dunes. The stronger the wind, the farther it can carry grains of sand before depositing them. Many Saharan sand dunes are of epic proportions and are always shifting, taking thousands of years to form.

A collection of dunes is called a dune field, and the largest dune fields are known as sand seas, or ergs.

SINGING SANDS

Sand dune landscapes aren't as silent as you might expect. Scientists have discovered a peculiar phenomenon: singing sand! A deep, echoing hum occurs when grains of sand slide down dune slopes. Stranger still is that each dune sings a slightly different tune.

TYPES OF SAND DUNE

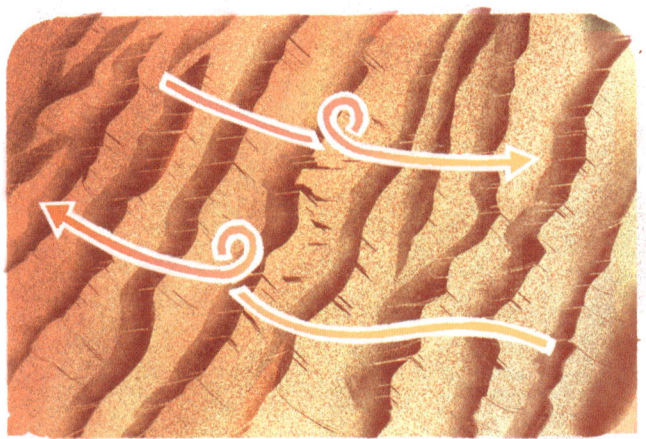

Linear dunes are made from wind blowing in from two directions. They are long, straight and run side by side.

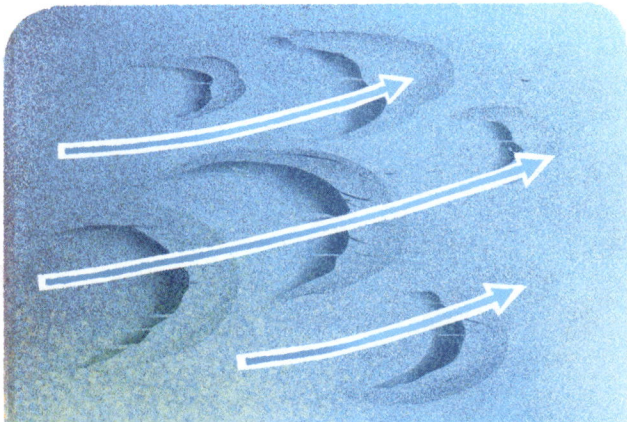

Crescent-shaped dunes are C-shaped and form in flat landscapes with winds coming from one direction.

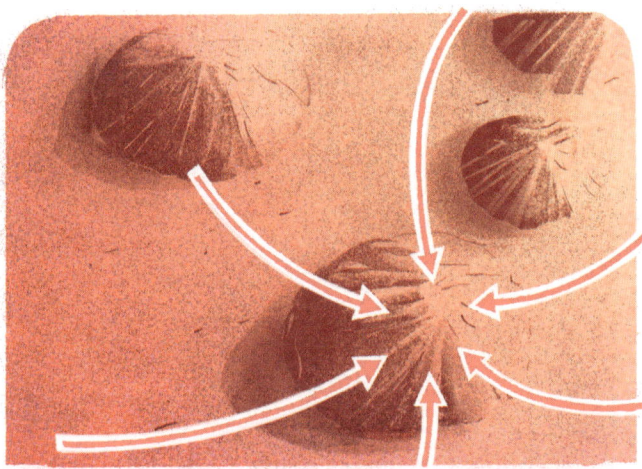

Dome dunes are circular-shaped and are produced when winds blow from all angles.

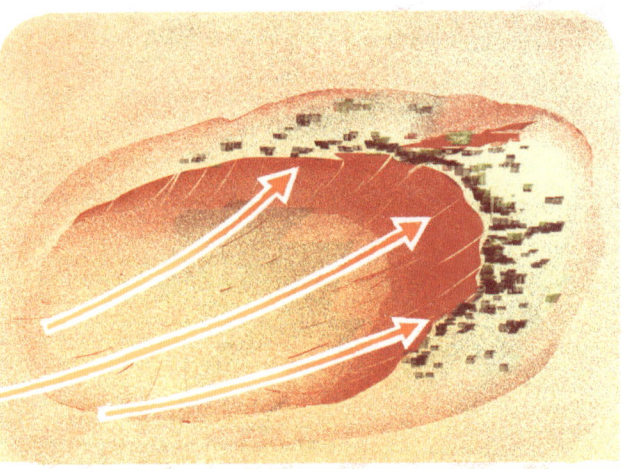

Blowout dunes form when wind hollows out the centre of the dune, often alongside vegetation.

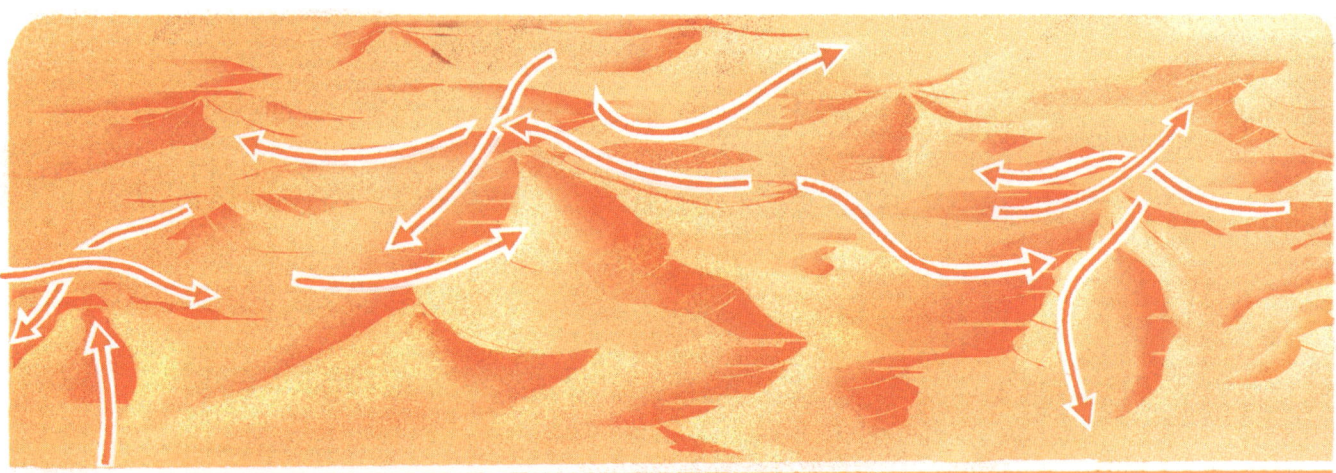

Star dunes are shaped by winds blowing in from multiple angles. They have star-like 'arms' that branch out from a peak. Most ergs are star dunes.

OASIS

An oasis is an area of land in a desert where water pools at the surface, whether natural or human-made. For desert dwellers and weary travellers, an oasis is a sanctuary. A place to drink water, rest and recuperate in shade away from the blistering sun. Without oases, life in the desert would not be possible.

This is how an oasis forms...

Step 1.

Showers tumble down the ridges of far-away mountains, and rushing torrents of flash floods cause rivers to spill over.

Step 2.

This water then seeps into the ground and flows along underground passageways, before being absorbed by rocks near the surface.

Some oasis water is referred to as 'fossil water'. It is non-renewable (it can't be replaced) and has been held in underground rocks for millions of years.

OASIS TOWNS

Because of the life-giving forces of desert oases, settlements have sprung up alongside them. Ouarzazate is the biggest oasis town in the Moroccan Sahara. It was an important hub between ancient trading routes, and it houses impressive kasbahs (fortresses) that have recently served as backdrops to several TV and film sets such as *Star Wars*.

Oasis water can travel long distances from its original source.

Step 3.

Finally, water oozes out of these rocks into an overground pool. Erosion or faults in the ground can also cause water to spill out at the surface.

WATERWAYS

Channels flow under, over and through the Sahara's otherwise dry landscape. Simple motor-pumps have been installed to pump huge quantities of water from beneath the ground.

NILE RIVER

The Nile courses through 11 countries over a distance of 6,600 km, making it the longest river in the world. It is essential for the livelihood of millions of people – not only does the river provide drinking water, it helps generate electricity, waters crops and enables transportation.

Egypt's Aswan Dam is one of the largest dams in the world. Dams control flooding, generate electricity and provide water for farming. However, their construction can also disrupt wildlife habitats and displace people from their homes.

Irrigation systems are a process of artificially watering plants. Water can be flooded into fields of crops or drip-fed through pipes to plant roots.

The Nile can't rely on sourcing water from the dry Sahara. Instead, its water is provided by tributaries in sub-Saharan Africa – the White Nile (coming from Uganda's Lake Victoria) and the Blue Nile (Ethiopia).

The Nile River

WADIS

Wadis are valleys and riverbeds in the Sahara that only flow during periods of heavy rainfall. Sudden flash floods gush through the hot landscape, carving out channels with their sheer force. These dry up until the rains come again – sometimes more than a year later.

LAKES

The 18 interconnected Lakes of Ounianga in Chad are fed by groundwater. They are the biggest and deepest lakes in the Sahara. Constant winds have caused 'wandering' sand dunes to zigzag in stripy patterns across the lakes.

EXTREME WEATHER

Though the Sahara is rarely visited by clouds and sees little rain, the weather here is anything but calm. Intense conditions can disrupt life for Saharan residents, and even those living on other continents!

Dust storms feed oceans and even the Amazon rainforest with nutrients. The aptly named 'Godzilla dust cloud' shrouded the Caribbean in a murky haze in 2020.

SAHARAN AIR LAYER

The Saharan Air Layer is a dense mass of hot air and dust particles up to 3 km thick that covers the desert. It whirls west over the Atlantic Ocean to the Americas every summer.

STORMY WEATHER

Dust and sandstorms occur when wind picks up dust from the ground and carries it in the air for miles. The Sahara Desert is the world's largest source of dust, and its dust storms can travel as far as South America. Sandstorms have larger particles that can cause more damage.

HABOOBS

A *haboob* (coming from the Arabic for wind) is a speeding dust storm that looks like a wall made of dust. Haboobs wreak havoc on towns and cities because visibility can drop to almost zero in a matter of minutes, causing power outages, aircraft collisions and damaging homes.

MISLEADING MIRAGES

Mirages are optical illusions, things that trick your vision and make you see things in the distance that aren't there. They often happen when looking out at hot, flat landscapes. They look realistic, but mysteriously disappear when you get closer. Mirages are caused by hot air meeting cooler air, which causes the light to bend, making us see things differently.

The most common mirage witnessed in the Sahara takes the form of a glinting pool of water.

DROMEDARY CAMEL

The dromedary or Arabian camel is one of the Sahara's most iconic symbols, and humans have been reliant on them for thousands of years. Many Saharans travel by truck today, but camels still have uses in these extreme conditions.

A group of camels is known as a caravan.

SHIPS OF THE DESERT

There are no wild camels in the Sahara. Dromedary camels were domesticated by humans 3,000 years ago. The camels are highly valued as modes of transport because they can carry goods and people weighing up to 450 kg for distances reaching 40 km a day. This has earned them the collective name 'ships of the desert'.

GOT THE HUMP

The dromedary camel is perfectly adapted to the landscape and weather conditions of the Sahara. The hump is the camel's most important asset. It is used to store fat reserves of up to 35 kg that are then broken down into a supply of energy and water. This allows them to travel long distances in dry conditions without water for weeks at a time.

Dromedary camels have one hump, while the Asian Bactrian camel has two.

Long legs and wide footpads help them to walk on sand without sinking.

Thick eyelashes and bushy eyebrows help keep sand out of their vision.

Tough lips and the insides of their mouths enable them to graze on spiky desert plants.

CAMEL RACING

For centuries, people of the Sahara have taken part in camel races. Over short distances the dromedary camel can reach a speed of 65 km per hour. It's taken very seriously – thousands of spectators and herders gather to watch and take part in competitive races across miles of desert landscape.

LIFE IN THE DUNES

From the surface, the sand dune landscape can appear quiet and deserted. But there are creatures of all sizes living here. Many have adapted their own unique survival skills to protect themselves from predators and the glare of the searing sun.

SPEEDY ANTS

One of the fastest insects on the planet is the Sahara silver ant, which can move 108 times its body length in a second! Their long legs and speedy strides prevent them from sinking into the sand or getting too hot. They also have special hairs that reflect sunlight to keep them cool. Silver ants leave their sandy nests for about 10 minutes at a time to search for food. They have to keep moving, though, or they risk being scorched by the sun.

SAND SWIMMER

The sandfish skink is a type of lizard that has the remarkable ability to swim through sand. It tucks its legs into its sides, dives in and propels itself forwards in a wriggly fish-like motion to move through the loose sand. With specially designed lungs that allow it to breathe beneath the sand, the sandfish inhales sand particles before it sneezes them out again.

Many desert animals are nocturnal. During the day, they take shelter in cool underground refuges beneath the sand, only coming out when it is colder at night.

FENNEC FOX

The fennec fox digs its own den to create a cocoon to sleep in during the day. This species of fox is best known for its distinctive big ears. This means it has excellent hearing, which is used to locate prey rustling below the thick layers of sand in the dark.

SAND BOA

The sand boa is a snake that has nostrils located high up on its head to help it detect prey when it is buried under the sand. At night it patiently lies in wait underground, ready to strike lizards, rodents and birds with its venomous fangs.

DEATHSTALKER SCORPION

This creature is one of the most dangerous species of scorpion in the world. It owes its name to a deadly venom that is released when threatened. It hides in burrows or beneath the shade of rocks during the day, and hunts for insects at night.

MOUNTAIN HIGHLANDS

The mountain ranges and highland regions of the Sahara are home to strong, agile creatures that are well-equipped to living in and around sheer cliffs and rocky terrain.

MONKEY BUSINESS

The Barbary macaque is the only primate found as far north as the Sahara Desert. They can withstand hot, dry summer months and cold, snowy winters at high altitudes. Many live in the cliffs, scrublands and forests of the Atlas Mountains.

HORNS AND HOOVES

Nubian ibex are nimble goats that roam steep mountainous clifftops. They boast majestic, curved horns that can grow up to 1.2 metres long.

Though they look like small rodents, the rock hyrax's closest relatives are actually elephants and manatees!

ROCK RABBITS

Commonly known as a rock rabbit, the rock hyrax is a cute and fluffy mammal that lives in mountain ranges such as the Hoggar Mountains of Algeria. They are well-suited to jumping and climbing the area's rugged terrain.

OASIS LIVING

The most important source of food and water in the Sahara is the lush, fertile oasis. Many animals live in or around oases and depend on them for their survival. Others visit for food and water and for a welcome break from the heat and aridity of the surrounding landscape.

The dorcas gazelle is a desert antelope that can go its entire life without drinking water, as it gets enough supply through the plants it eats.

WATERING HOLE

Migratory birds, such as the desert warbler and the Saharan cisticola, rely on oases habitats during their long southward journeys. They stop to drink water and feed on seeds, insects and the nectar and fruit provided by oasis plants. Desert tortoises can go weeks without food or water, and then they can drink up to 15 per cent of their body weight to keep them going.

TREE OF LIFE

The resilient date palm is one of the few plants that truly thrives in the Sahara, surviving daytime temperatures of 25 to 50°C. It is called the 'tree of life' because it produces the date fruit, which is a huge resource for local diets and the farming industry. Date palm forests have been planted by humans in oases because their roots need the water supply and their leaves need the sun to grow.

In the shade of date palms grow other fruit trees such as oranges, olives, figs, pomegranates and peaches.

NILE RIVER

The Nile River is full of life. Many types of flora (plants) and fauna (wildlife) fill its waters and riverbanks. Growing along the fertile banks are an abundance of tropical plants, from banana trees to bamboo and the papyrus plant. In the river swim hippos, the Nile crocodile and more than 800 species of fish.

African fish eagle

BIRDLIFE

Perched along the riverbanks are storks, flamingos, pelicans and herons. Swooping to catch fish are African fish eagles. Bobbing on the water are Egyptian geese, often depicted on Ancient Egyptian emblems.

Shoebill stork

The Egyptian goose has distinctive dark-brown patches around its eyes.

Catfish

Perch

Elephant-snout fish

SOFTSHELL TURTLE

The softshell turtle's shell lacks the hard, bony plates belonging to most turtles. Its flattened, streamlined shell enables it to move swiftly through the river.

RIVER CROCS

The fierce Nile crocodile is the river's top predator. They are excellent swimmers and can hold their breath for up to two hours underwater. Growing up to a whopping 6 metres in length, this croc is one of the largest species in the world, and they are equally as ferocious – their bite force is one of the most powerful in the animal kingdom.

Female Nile crocodiles dig a nest on the riverbank where they lay dozens of eggs.

HIPPOS

Hippos are found in the Al-Sudd and southern regions of the Nile. They spend most of their lives in the water, but also live on land.

Adult male ostriches can reach a height of 2.8 metres.

In the wild, giant tortoises shelter in burrows, and can live for up to 70 years.

GRASSLANDS

The Sahara's pastures are home to some mighty creatures – the open landscape means these animals need to be tough to survive!

BIG CAT

The Saharan or Northwest African cheetah is found in the Sahara and neighbouring Sahel region. They have a lighter shade of fur than other species of cheetah, as their sandy colouring helps them blend into the desert environment. Sadly, the Saharan cheetah is one of the most endangered big cats in the world, with an estimated population of 250.

LONG-LEGGED BIRD

The North African ostrich, or red-necked ostrich, is a large bird that roams Sahara regions from Morocco to Sudan. Though it can't fly, it has long, strong legs that help it reach a speed of 72 km an hour, making it one of the fastest land-dwelling creatures on the planet.

GIANT TORTOISE

The largest species of mainland tortoise in the world is the African spurred tortoise. It can grow up to 80 cm in length and weigh more than 45 kg. Their thick skin protects them from prey and the desert heat.

LAKES

Most lakes that once existed in the Sahara dried up long ago, and there are very few that remain. There are 18 interconnected lakes at Ounianga in northeastern Chad, and together they make up the largest permanent freshwater lake system in a desert on the planet. The water is supplied from huge underground springs – without these, the lakes would evaporate due to the heat and lack of rainfall.

Around 10,000 years ago, the lakes were connected, and made up one huge pool.

The biggest and deepest is Lake Yoa.

Many of the Ounianga lakes are covered by a sheet of floating reeds. This protective layer prevents too much of the water from evaporating.

SALTY WATER

The lakes are home to wildlife such as tilapia, toads and birds that pass through, such as the greater flamingo and white pelican. A few lakes have a high concentration of salt water – some with even more than the sea! Birds feed off the algae at these pools before flying off to wash the salt water from their feathers in the freshwater lakes.

SECRET GARDEN

Nestled in the rocky plateaus of northeastern Chad is the Ennedi Massif. Sheltered from the rest of the world for thousands of years, this green paradise is a sanctuary for humans, animals and plant life. More than 500 species of plants flourish here; these and the water supply attract wildlife such as the desert hedgehog, Barbary sheep, dorcas gazelle, striped hyena, caracal and patas monkey.

The West African crocodiles that live in the Guelta d'Archei are one of the last remaining groups of the species that scientists know to still exist in the Sahara.

DUNG DIET

Guelta d'Archei is a pool of water in Ennedi where crocodiles, fish, frogs and algae share a habitat. Because camels stop here to drink, the guelta is filled with camel dung that has turned the water dark! It is now part of the food chain – the algae thrive on the dung, the fish feed on the algae, and in turn the crocodiles feed on the fish.

BOUNTIFUL BIRDS

Ennedi sees more than 185 species of birds stopping for sustenance on their long migration voyages, such the Sudan golden sparrow, known for its brilliant yellow plumage. The first study of birdlife at Ennedi took place as recently as 2019, so there could well be lots more to discover!

The cave paintings show how the Sahara climate has changed over the years - the oldest cave paintings illustrate cattle, but the slightly more recent paintings feature camels.

WHAT CAVE PAINTINGS TELL US

Preserved in the canyons and caves of Ennedi is rock art made by prehistoric hunter-gatherers. They are illustrated relics of the animals that used to live here - from giraffes to rhinos and elephants, and even livestock such as cows and horses. People owning livestock suggests that there was once more rainfall here, as mammals such as cows and horses need more water and food supplies to survive than animals such as camels.

LEGEND OF THE ENNEDI TIGER

Prowling the moonlit plains of remotest Chad is rumoured to be a fanged beast. A ferocious creature believed to have gone extinct thousands of years ago, until now...

Some say it is larger than a lion, with fangs as big as walrus tusks. Others recall its shaggy coat of red-and-white stripes. Sometimes the beast is spotted near water. At other times it is seen lurking in the Ennedi mountains. There are even those who claim it is followed by a trail of butterflies, flitting and twirling in its wake. Witnesses agree on one thing only: this creature is an ancient African sabretooth cat thought to have perished during the last Ice Age. Local people have named it the Ennedi tiger, or *hadjel*.

At night, the tiger leaves its darkened cave to hunt by the light of the moon. The morning light brings discoveries of animal remains punctured with mysterious fang-shaped wounds. To this day, sightings of the Ennedi tiger are reported by travellers and locals alike. But are they mere legends? Or has the tiger evaded detection, skulking in the shadowy corners of the Sahara for centuries?

PEOPLE AND COMMUNITIES

PREHISTORIC COMMUNITIES

The earliest remains of Homo sapiens (humans) ever found were discovered in the Moroccan Sahara. An excavation in 2017 uncovered teeth, bones and stone tools estimated to be 300,000 years old. This breakthrough challenges the widespread belief that East Africa is the birthplace of humanity.

HUMAN TRACES

Human-made clues left behind can teach us about how ancient peoples lived, from what they ate to how they hunted. Stone tools, weapons and rock art reveal that early humans were hunter-gatherers and fisherfolk.

HUNTERS

The Aterian civilisation existed across North Africa during the Middle Stone Age. Known for their finely crafted stone tools, they were also one of the first cultures to use the bow and arrow.

FISHERFOLK

The Kiffians lived in what is now Mauritania and Mali, when the Sahara region was at its wettest. They were expert hunters, believed to be one of the first cultures in Africa to fish, using harpoons to catch fish, hippos and crocodiles.

FARMERS

Based in Tunisia and Algeria, the Capsian civilisation was one of the earliest to farm. They used flint tools that were often embellished with patterns, and made decorative art such as shell and bone ornaments.

HERDERS

The Tenerians were skilled cattle herders from Niger. They held burial practices that included offerings such as ostrich eggshells, jewellery and ceramics.

ANCIENT COMMUNITIES

The Sahara was a thoroughfare that connected different civilisations, making it the perfect spot for cultures to meet, and for empires to battle.

CARTHAGE

Strategically situated on the Mediterranean Sea in modern-day Tunisia, Ancient Carthage was a seafaring city that traded goods between Europe and Africa. It controlled a huge territory that included parts of Europe, and it rivalled Ancient Rome. Three great battles between Carthage and Rome took place, known as the Punic Wars.

Ancient Carthage used war elephants to drive the Roman army back towards the sea.

NUMIDIA

The Numidian Empire ruled over modern-day Algeria and parts of Tunisia. Famed for their horseback-riding skills, the Numidians were made up of various Berber tribes united by a king. They teamed up with the Romans to destroy the city of Carthage, and later turned against Rome and lost.

ANCIENT EGYPT

Ancient Egypt rose up along the fertile banks of the Nile. Here was a land of majestic pyramids, ornate temples and powerful pharaohs (kings and queens). Spanning 3,000 years, this was one of the most influential civilisations in human history. The Egyptians made incredible advances in language, astronomy, mathematics, science, medicine and engineering.

Hieroglyphics

The Ancient Egyptians were one of the first civilisations to develop a form of writing. Instead of letters, the language used pictograms (symbols and images) called hieroglyphs. People would inscribe these on papyrus paper.

Mummification

An Ancient Egyptian ritual to preserve bodies was called mummification. This involved removing moisture from the body and then wrapping it in linen. They believed this would allow people to pass over into the afterlife and live forever.

Gods and Goddesses

More than 2,000 gods and goddesses feature in Ancient Egyptian myths. Many were depicted with human bodies and animal heads. Ra, god of the sun, has the head of a hawk, while Anubis, god of the afterlife, has a jackal's head.

PASTORAL NOMADS

The Sahara has the highest rates of urbanisation in Africa, which means citizens increasingly reside in towns and cities. However, many nomads still thrive, and each group has its own traditions that have been shaped by the desert. They are attached to a given territory, or pastures, and many own houses in settlements. Select family members travel to find good pasture.

Excluding the Nile Valley, roughly 2.5 million people currently live in the Sahara.

THE BLUE PEOPLE

The Tuareg are a group of Berbers who use indigo ink to dye their robes a deep blue, earning them the name, the 'blue people'. They travel with herds of camels, sheep and goats, and build tents out of sticks, mats and animal skins. The Tuareg have a long history of music and poetry. A traditional instrument called an *imzad* is made from a gourd fruit and has a single horsehair string.

DESERT DWELLERS

The term Bedouin comes from the Arabic for 'desert dweller'. The Bedouin people are Arabic-speaking nomads of the Middle East and North Africa who traditionally bred animals such as Arabian horses. These prized possessions would sleep in their masters' tents at night to prevent them from being stolen. Other Bedouin customs include sword dancing, poetry and weaving.

LEGEND OF QUEEN TIN HINAN OF THE TUAREG

There was once a powerful queen of the desert nomads. Her name was Tin Hinan, or 'She of the Tents'. Though her story was believed to be legend, it ends with a real-life discovery.

During the Middle Ages, some women ruled over the people of North Africa. One such leader was Queen Tin Hinan. Banished from the northern Sahara, she led her followers south, eventually settling in the Hoggar Mountains of Algeria. There, she founded and governed the Tuareg.

Centuries later in 1925, archaeologists in Algeria discovered a majestic stone tomb. It sat perched on a hill overlooking the meeting of two wadis. The tomb had only one entrance, but many rooms. Inside, the explorers found towering mounds of treasure glinting in the dim light. There were jewels and coins and precious stones. Among it all lay a skeleton of a woman once buried in splendour. On her right forearm were seven bracelets made of silver, and on her left, seven made of gold. She was surrounded by luxurious offerings, from sparkling glass goblets to arrowheads sculpted from iron. Could this have been the final resting place of the mythical Queen Tin Hinan?

During the expedition a fierce thunderstorm broke out. Rain erupted from the skies and cascaded down the mountains. To the Tuaregs, this was the work of angry *djinn* spirits. Made up of smokeless flames, they dwell in the earth and air and delight in punishing humans. Furious that the queen's rest had been disturbed, they were keen to seek their revenge.

NOMADIC TRADITIONS

Welcoming guests into their homes is important to nomadic communities. They cook over open fires and sleep in tents under the stars. Wherever they make a base, an extra tent will be put up for guests. When you are used to travelling in an inhospitable environment, a shelter is essential and home comforts appreciated.

THE FREE PEOPLE

The Berbers have inhabited many countries in North Africa for thousands of years. They are also known as Imazighen, which means 'free people'. Berbers used to make everything they needed from natural materials. Clay would form ceramics, while leather, wool and *kilim* (woven tapestry) made rugs and clothes. Berbers still invite travellers to share a meal with them and stay in their tents.

PEOPLE OF THE SAHARA

The Sahrawi are of mixed Berber, Arab and sub-Saharan African descent. Their name translates from Arabic as 'of the Sahara'. They live in and around the Western Sahara region and are recognised by their vibrant robes and headscarves. *Karum* means hospitality, which is important in Sahrawi culture. For instance, it can involve a complex tea-making ritual for guests that can take hours to prepare.

WESTERN SAHARA CONFLICT

While neighbouring Morocco claims the Western Sahara as its own, Algeria and the Sahrawi Arab Democratic Republic fight for its independence. As a result of the conflict, many Sahrawi people have fled their homes and live in refugee camps. A peace movement still works to end the dispute for good.

SAHARA EXPLORERS

The Saharan landscape challenged even well-prepared explorers, and many lost their lives due to harsh weather, diseases, bandits and conflicts with locals. This didn't deter them, however, and by the 19th century expeditions were booming.

Caillié travelled the River Niger on a goods vessel. It was part of a 50-strong fleet, which helped provide protection against bandits.

1351   **1793**   **1827**

FINDING GOLD

Often compared to Marco Polo, Ibn Battuta travelled to more than 40 countries over three decades. Trekking over the Atlas Mountains from Morocco, Battuta found hospitality among fellow Muslims, from whom he bought camels for his onward journey. He rode to the Western Sahara and the Kingdom of Mali, where he witnessed its ample gold supply.

POSITIVE PRAISE

William George Browne joined an annual camel caravan route travelling from Egypt to Sudan. Over two intrepid Sahara crossings, he withstood disease, murder attempts and an arrest by the sultan of Darfur, yet Browne wrote positively about the customs of North African culture compared with Europe.

UNDER COVER

Born to poor parents who died young, Auguste René Caillié left home at 16 and became the first European to return from Timbuktu alive. Caillié often travelled alone, famously disguising himself as a local, and funded his trips by working in Africa. To prepare, he spent years living with locals, learning Arabic and embracing Islam.

1850   1869   1933

THE SCHOLAR

Johann Heinrich Barth was the first European explorer to examine the Sahara from a truly scholarly perspective, and his work was referenced by Darwin. Barth became fluent in Arabic and local languages and formed friendships with African rulers, one of whom rescued him from a kidnapping.

TRAGIC CROSSING

Pioneering photographer Alexine Tinne was the first European woman to attempt crossing the Sahara. Together with a team of natural scientists, Tinne studied plants, and made maps and surveys of the land. She set out with Tuareg camel drivers to cross the desert, but tragedy struck as she came into conflict and was killed before finishing the journey.

FAILURE AND SUCCESS

László Almásy made many failed attempts to locate the hidden oasis of Zerzura. However, in 1933 Almásy and his team did discover something – an important prehistoric rock art site that suggested the Sahara had not always been a desert. Almásy named it the 'Cave of Swimmers'.

TRANS-SAHARAN TRADE ROUTES

An ancient transportation network once criss-crossed the Sahara for thousands of miles. Merchants, traders and travellers would journey across the desert on camels, carrying goods to exchange such as salt, gold, ivory and textiles. The routes were largely controlled by Tuareg, Arab and Tubu groups. Goods were transported overseas from port cities such as Tunis and Cairo, and major trading towns boomed.

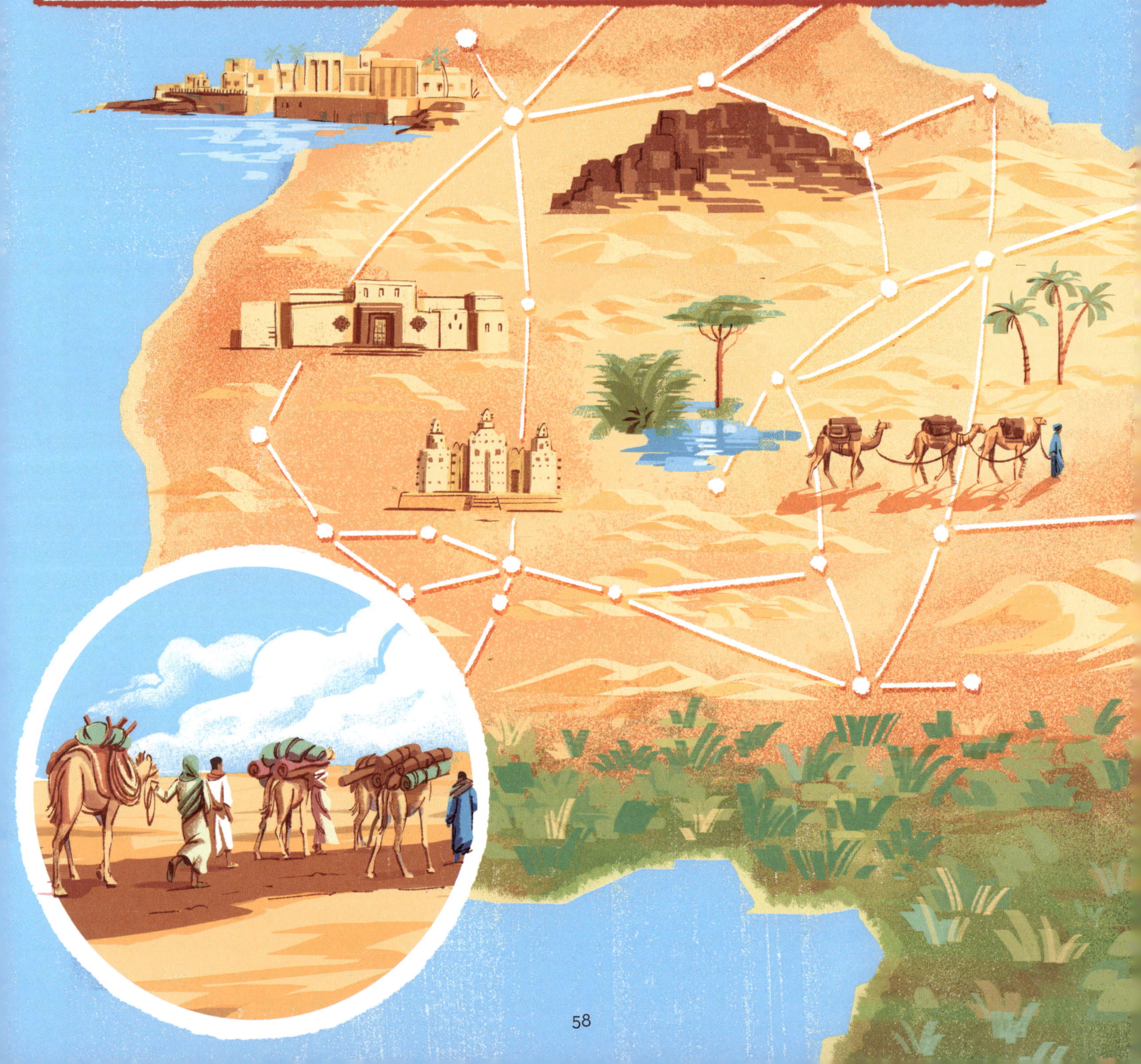

SPREAD THE WORD

Because the trade route connected people from different places, it contributed to the spread of cultures, languages and ideas. The network played a significant role in the expansion of religion, as often business transactions would lead to Islamic merchants converting local populations to their belief system.

BEWARE OF BANDITS

If you were trading expensive goods, you'd have to keep an eye out for gangs of bandits. Typically, these thieves and conmen were outlaws (lawbreakers) operating in isolated areas with very few authorities.

WORTH ITS WEIGHT IN GOLD

Though gold is far more expensive than salt today, the two were traded for one another, and together made up the majority of long-distance trade. Gold was abundant in West and Central Africa, and salt was considered precious as it was hard to come by.

SAHARAN SLAVE TRADE

The trade route also played a part in slavery for hundreds of years until the late 19th century. Sub-Saharan Africans were captured during raids or wars, and then forced to travel across the Sahara by camel caravan. Brutal conditions meant that many would die during the journey. Those who did survive were sold like goods at market and put to work as labourers with no rights or means of escape.

TIMBUKTU

The Malian town of Timbuktu was an important centre of trade and learning. Its rich cultural heritage is made up of African, Arab and Islamic influences. Housed here are some of the oldest mosques in Africa, and one of the first universities in the world, all built from mud bricks. The most profitable items traded in Timbuktu were books, as owning them was a sign of wealth. Books were so sought after that a king is said to have bought a dictionary for the price of two horses!

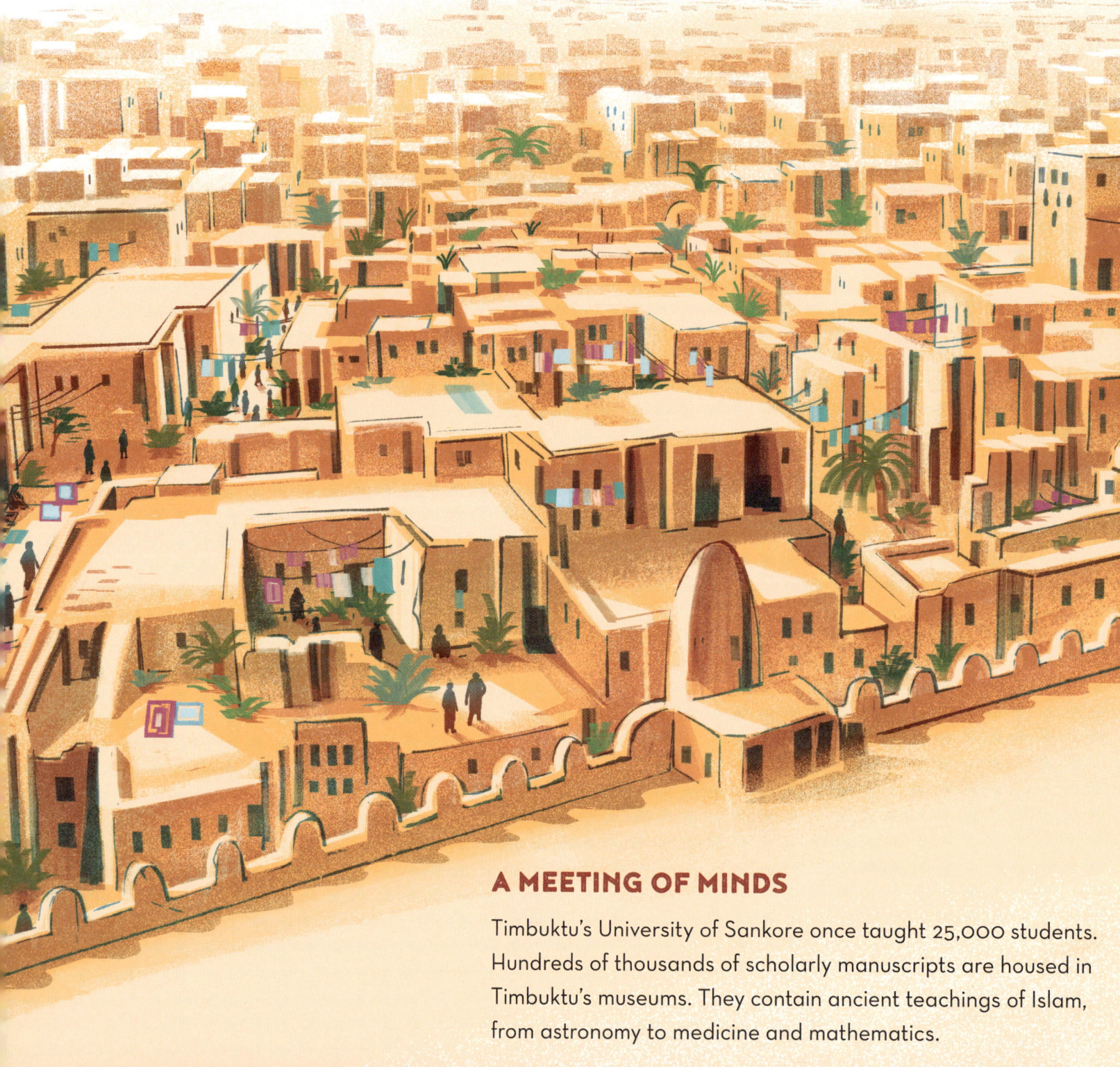

A MEETING OF MINDS

Timbuktu's University of Sankore once taught 25,000 students. Hundreds of thousands of scholarly manuscripts are housed in Timbuktu's museums. They contain ancient teachings of Islam, from astronomy to medicine and mathematics.

SINKING SAND

Timbuktu's mud-and-timber mosques, roads and buildings are in danger of being taken over by the sand from the desert. Wind erosion and desertification (land turning into desert) caused by climate change has caused sand to pile up. Efforts are underway to maintain buildings and preserve the mud-brick monuments.

WHAT'S IN A NAME?

For centuries, Europeans had learned about the teachings and trading of the city. As they struggled to reach it via the Sahara Desert, Timbuktu became a faraway place of myth. This is where the phrase 'from here to Timbuktu' comes from.

LOST CITY OF ZERZURA

Late at night in the desert, you may hear campfire tales about the lost city of Zerzura. They tell of a magical oasis settlement hidden somewhere west of the Nile...

Long ago, a camel herder survived a sandstorm that had swept through the desert for seven days. While he was searching for water, he stumbled upon a group of men who offered to take him back to their home. Thankful for their kindness, he followed them over great stretches of sand. At long last, they arrived at a walled city the men called 'Zerzura'. Carved into the city's gates was a small bird, and in its beak a key. The men used it to enter, and the camel herder delighted

at the sights within. People came and went from luxurious white houses, springs flowed, and golden treasures spilled from every surface. In a castle lay a sleeping king and queen who reigned over the city from their slumber.

One moonless night, the camel herder crept away. Months later, he landed on the shores of Benghazi. When Benghazi's ruler, the Emir, heard the man's story, he wondered why anyone would leave such an enchanting place. He ordered his guards to search the camel herder's belongings, and they found a ruby ring stolen from Zerzura. The Emir had never seen such a magnificent jewel, and so he and his men left in search of the fabled city. They returned empty handed, without a tale to tell, and Zerzura was once again lost to the sands of time.

DINOSAUR BATTLES

If you visited the Sahara 100 million years ago, you'd see huge reptiles soaring in the sky, giant turtles floating down rivers and predatory dinosaurs stomping through vast grasslands. Every year new findings excavated by palaeontologists (fossil scientists) help piece together information about these now-extinct creatures.

BIG BONES

The largest carnivorous dinosaur ever found is the Spinosaurus. In Morocco in 2014 its skeleton was found almost intact – all 11 metres of it! It's also considered to be the earliest discovered semi-aquatic dinosaur.

SEA MONSTERS

A huge sea once flowed in from the Tethys and split the Sahara in two. It was teeming with gigantic sea monsters. Fossils found in Mali include huge catfish and elongated sea snakes that once swam among tangled mangrove forests.

MOUTH MACHINE

Bones belonging to the plant-eating Nigersaurus have recently been dug up in Niger. They reveal an unusual-shaped mouth designed to vacuum up tough plants, and more than 500 teeth to help with chewing!

SUPERCROC

A fossil graveyard is buried within a Niger valley called Gadoufaoua – meaning 'the place where camels fear to go'. When its rivers dried up, fossils were preserved in their banks, including a huge marine mammal known as 'supercroc'. Distantly related to today's crocodiles, it weighed between eight and 10 tonnes. A super croc indeed.

Modern croc skull

Supercroc skull

GREEN SAHARA

It might be difficult to believe that human life has existed in the Sahara for millennia, but it was not always such a harsh environment. Scientists refer to the last humid period as the 'Green Sahara'. During this time the region experienced increased rainfall. There were rainforests and marshes, lakes and wetlands. Mountains were sprinkled with lime, oak and oleander trees.

CAVE OF SWIMMERS

Discoveries of rock carvings called petroglyphs give us a hint of how prehistoric civilisations thrived in a milder climate. Archaeologists have discovered petroglyphs at Gilf Kebir in Egypt. One has earned the name 'Cave of Swimmers' because the carvings depict human figures that look like they're swimming! It is just one of many clues that suggest there was once more water in the Sahara.

ENDINGS AND BEGINNINGS

Around 5,500 years ago the desertification of the Sahara marked the end of the Green Sahara. People and animals were forced to move elsewhere in search of a greater supply of food and water. Others remained and adapted to the effects of climate change over the centuries.

ANIMALS GALORE

Wildlife that has since moved south of the Sahara was once in abundance. Hippos splashed about in rivers, lions stalked gazelle and giraffe in grasslands, monkeys swung from forest treetops and herds of elephants gathered at the many watering holes. Some animals are now extinct due to habitat loss or hunting.

TODAY AND BEYOND

Our use of things like petrol and coal are causing the Earth to get warmer much more rapidly than is natural, making places like the Sahara more difficult to live in. High temperatures also cause more of the sea to evaporate and then rain down, resulting in dangerous flash floods.

SAHARA FROM SPACE

Earth observation satellites in space monitor changes to the landscape. In the last 100 years they have noted that the Sahara's range has spread a further 10 per cent due to human and natural causes.

CONSERVATION INITIATIVES

There are efforts in place to help tackle climate change and prevent the Sahara and surrounding areas from becoming inhospitable.

Sahara Forest Project

Already successful in a number of the Middle East's desert nations, this project wants to make the Sahara eco-friendlier by using a magic ingredient: seawater. Seawater greenhouses can produce renewable energy, increase the fresh water supply and enable crops to grow in dry areas that can't naturally sustain farming.

Solar power project

Morocco is a beacon for solar power technology. Taking advantage of high levels of sunshine in the Moroccan Sahara is Noor-Ouarzazate, the world's largest concentrated solar power plant used to generate electricity. It has reduced fossil fuels and provided jobs for the local community, and there are plans underway to install more plants.

SAVING THE SAHARA

Now you know that the Sahara is not just a sandy desert, but one of constant change. A place of monsoons and dry stretches, evolving animals and different rulers. We have unearthed buried bones and treasures that tell us about its varied past, and there are many more secrets waiting to be discovered.

Though the resilient have survived, life in the Sahara is threatened. Temperatures rise to impossible extremes, and more frequent downpours burst from the skies. If this continues, the people and animals of the Sahara will be driven out, leaving this vast land as barren as the moon.

Though we're not all navigating the desert, we are each responsible for keeping the Earth's ecosystems balanced. As we have seen, nature can flourish where we enable it. By being friendlier to the planet, humans can help sustain life in the Sahara for years to come.

GLOSSARY

Agriculture: Practice of growing crops and farming.

Apex predators: Animals at the top of the food chain.

Archaeologists: People who study things left behind from the past.

Arid: Extremely dry conditions that lack rainfall and humidity.

Barren: Landscapes that are absent of life or produce few plants.

Burial offerings: Ritual of burying goods alongside the deceased as gifts to gods or items to be carried into the afterlife.

Camel caravan: Large groups of camels led by people across the desert.

Climate change: Changes in average weather, temperature and climate that have been influenced by human activity.

Desertification: When fertile land becomes a desert over time.

Domesticate: To be tamed by humans.

Drought: Prolonged period of low rainfall that causes the land to dry up.

Ecosystem: Community of all the living things in a place, and the non-living environment around them.

Erosion: Gradual wearing away of a material, such as land worn away by the wind or sea.

Evaporation process: A liquid changing into a gas, particularly by being heated.

Excavate: Removing buried remains from the ground.

Extinct: When an entire species or type of animal dies out.

Flash flood: Sudden, often extreme, local flooding, often due to heavy rain.

Freshwater: Natural water from an inland body such as a lake, as opposed to seawater.

Hieroglyphics: Form of written language, made up of symbols and signs, used in Ancient Egypt.

Humid: When air has a high level of moisture.

Hunter-gatherer: People who hunt, fish, forage and harvest wild food.

Irrigation: Supply of water to land or crops to aid growth.

Islam: Religion that follows the teachings of Allah, His prophet Muhammad and the Qur'an holy book. Followers are called Muslims.

Kasbah: Fortress or citadel in North Africa.

Livestock: Animals kept by people and used for their assets such as milk or meat.

Manuscript: Book or document written by hand.

Merchant: Person who buys, trades and sells goods for a profit.

Migration: The seasonal movement of animals from one area to another, for feeding or breeding purposes.

Mirage: Illusion caused by the bending of light that makes people see imaginary things reflected on the ground in the distance.

Mosque: Islamic building used for worship.

Mummification: Custom of preserving a deceased body.

Natives: Living beings born to a certain area.

Nocturnal: Being active at night and usually sleeping during the day.

Nomads: People who have no fixed home and wander from place to place.

Oasis: Fertile area of a desert enabled by a source of water.

Pharaoh: Ancient Egyptian ruler.

Prehistoric: The time before written history.

Pyramid: Huge monument with a square base and four triangular sides that reach a singular point.

Sand dune: Mound or ridge of sand shaped by the wind.

Scholar: Highly educated person who has done advanced study in a special area.

Tomb: Burial chamber for the deceased.

Trade: Business of buying, selling and exchanging items.

Wadi: Dry valley or stream that fills with water in the rainy season.

INDEX

WRITTEN BY CHRISTINA WEBB

Christina Webb is a writer and editor with a passion for diverse storytelling and a soft spot for unusual animals. She holds a BA in English Literature and an MA in Creative Writing from the University of Surrey. After a decade in London, she now lives in one of England's oldest towns, Abingdon-on-Thames. You'll likely find her curled up with a book, cultivating a wildlife-friendly garden or following her itchy feet to exciting new places.

ILLUSTRATED BY MUTI

MUTI is a creative studio founded in 2011 and is based in the city of Cape Town, South Africa. Their team of dedicated illustrators and animators produce inspiring and original artwork from their studio, at the foot of the majestic Table Mountain. If they're not drawing beautiful pictures you might find them surfing in the chilly waters of False Bay, hiking in the Cederberg, or cooking on an open flame with an icy beverage in hand.

WITH EXPERT HELP FROM

Judith Scheele

Judith Scheele is a social anthropologist who has spent many years travelling in the Sahara, on the back of bumpy trucks, in transborder trading posts, dusty manuscript libraries, camel camps and shady oasis gardens. She currently lives and teaches in Marseille, in southern France.

ALSO IN THE SERIES

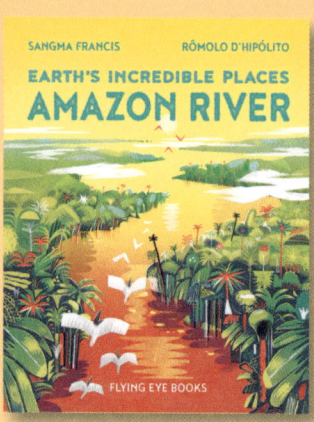

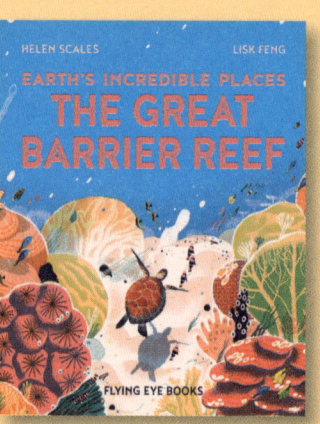

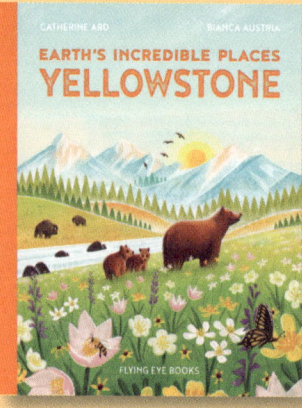

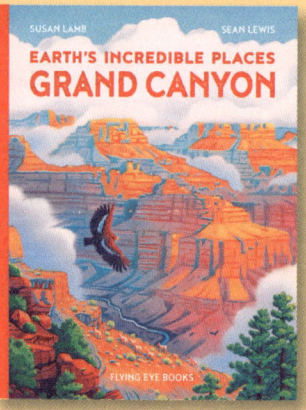

WWW.FLYINGEYEBOOKS.COM